Bare Witness:
Mask Off

Authored by Krystal Carr

Bare Witness:
Mask Off
Copyright © 2019 by Krystal Carr

All rights reserved. No part of this book may be reproduced or transmitted in any form or by any means without written permission from the author.

Disclaimer: Various versions of the Bible were used in the production of this literary work KJV, NKJV, NLT, MSG.

ISBN (978-1-7335709-3-0)

Table of Contents

Dedication iv

Foreword v

Introduction vi

Chapters

1:   Go Girl, It's Ya Birthday! 1

2:   Looking for Love 10

3:   Hooking Up with Lust 21

4:   Trying to *Right* my *Wrongs* 34

5:   *Loving* Mr. Wrong, *Again* 47

6:   Death Was the Necessary Part 57

7:   Life *After* Death 72

8:   Life *Is* Purposed, Purpose *Is* Life 84

About the Author 98

<u>Dedication</u>

"Bare Witness," is dedicated to my beloved children...

Keyana, thank you for your gentleness and your ever-loving heart. I love the mother *you are*, continue pursuing the best for your life. I love you to infinity.

Keiton, thank you for accepting my guidance that helped smooth-out your rough edges. You are an unconfessed momma's boy; your dreams are closer than you think! Just stretch a little further to pull them into your reach. I love you boy!

To my baby boy Dewayne, thank you for being attentive when I "preached" to you, for making yourself available when I needed you, and encouraging me when I didn't have the words or strength to encourage myself. I love you eternally and I miss you, *always*!

This narrated truth was written for individuals who have loved and lost… to those who have lost themselves while searching and those who have found themselves in Christ… Understand He gives us the strength to discover the empowerment of a "Bare(d) Witness…" God's truth about you *is* your identity!

<u>Foreword</u>

The audaciousness to bear our souls is frightening, but the truth is the most liberating aspect of ourselves. Consequently, when "our truths" are confined by shame, guilt, other people's opinions, but more importantly US... the freeing supremacy of the truth is NOT released.

Krystal Carr has penned a poignant, compelling, and bare truth about her shortcomings, disappointments, epiphanies, and victories! "Bare Witness" opens the door to the closets in her life. Ironically, when she told the secrets and revealed the skeletons, she was unashamed! While working with Krystal, this reality met me face to face... the paths we travel in life are not an indication of God being ABSENT from our lives... but it is a BLATANT sign of Him being PRESENT in our lives.

Too often, we view our lives as dismal, unfair, and more commonly uncertain... *but* we are purpose(d) to be here! Fortunately, the paths we travel serve as the molding agents of our calling, so that we ultimately understand why we *were* chosen! Allow this unfiltered account of Ms. Carr's life journey [thus far], to educate you, encourage you, but more than anything – empower you to be a "Bare Witness!"

Grace & Peace,

Victoria Holmes
Literary Impressions
Chief Editor & Literary Coach

Introduction

Silent tears, stained pillows, always seeing, but never knowing, and always misunderstood. But he loves me, they loved me, however... they never *knew* me. Sick, nauseous, poisonous, hazardous to my health, they were toxic! As I thought I should, I swallowed the poison and endured the sickness because I thought it was love. I am Krystal, and I believed in the faux pas love. I played the game, "He loves me, he loves me not... He loves me, he loves me not!" But did I love me? I think not... so now I am here as a "Bare Witness."

"What's not clicking up there? Do you ever think? I've been waiting while you were galivanting. DON'T LET THIS HAPPEN AGAIN! I don't have time for this, and I don't have time for you either." I stood there, quietly flabbergasted, embarrassed, and questionably afraid, not of him but what I anticipated would develop. Toxic relationship(s). No, I'm not speaking of "us", but I'm talking about me, myself, and, I. I accepted the poison, I swallowed their pride and regurgitated *their* insecurity as my own... low self-esteem, depression, inadequacy, self- hatred, self-loathing. "Killing me softly with *this* song, telling my whole life with *their* words" 🎶(sing Lauryn) miseducation of me.

EPIPHANY. I finally looked in the mirror and recognized who I had become versus who I should be and who I was created to be. HE made me fearfully and wonderfully. HE knows all of it, but I failed to recognize HIS glory in me so I settled for what I thought it should be and not for what "it" was created to be. This "it" was *love (faux pas- imitation, fake, not genuine "love" behavior that is socially mistaken yet socially acceptable as it actually draws one away from true love)*, love was impatient, love was hurtful, love was scornfully jealous, love was obsessive, love was unfaithful, love held me "at fault," and love never truthfully loved me back.

AGAPE, this will be an everlasting LOVE 🎵" (sang Natalie)! LOVE is patient, LOVE is kind, LOVE is uplifting, LOVE is liberating, LOVE takes the blame and keeps no record of my wrong(s). My LOVE always protects, it is always trustworthy, and it will never forsake YOU… Yours Truly, ~ God.

...Because of this I can now BARE WITNESS!

Chapter 1
"Go Girl, It's Ya Birthday"
Case No. 77-120300FL
(Pivotal Point #1- December 03, 1977)

ARRAIGNMENT. According to previous testimony, the defendants/parents of Krystal Carr, two juveniles - ages 16 and 19 developed and expressed "love" for each other. They went to great lengths to see each other, even when it was against their parents' admonishing. Frequently, they utilized the friendships of their siblings to manipulate the connection of the forbidden relationship. Being affected by lascivious thoughts, unexplainable feelings, and raging hormones they had no idea what was happening between them. Was this an interest? Was this chemistry? Was this "love"? Or was this just two curious teens experiencing a seemingly insatiable attraction they didn't quite understand and were not equipped to manage, contain, or restrain. Ultimately, these feelings drew them to a place that could not be reconciled by physical connections. They were overtaken by feelings of sexual attraction and a form of "love", these two engaged in marital rights without the law. Their bond was lustfully consecrated and led to the loss of their innocence, purity, identity, and purpose. Innocence lost, because of actions that caused a bond that locked in a futile understanding of the world and life views sustained by ignorance. Purity of the body, soul, and spirit now dirty because they were given away for a feeling instead of a holy/wholly connection.

    Identity interrupted, as the intertwining of two underdeveloped psyches are fused together as one. Their purposes were postponed, as it was choked out by misinterpreted love that manifested as much more than lust. Now without knowing, they initiated a generational cycle of teenage pregnancy, rejection, promiscuity, low self-esteem, self-doubt, unworthiness, and an impoverished mindset to settle for less than God's best to continue.

[Side note]: *Pay attention to the cycles and patterns in your family. Especially, if they don't show growth. Just because it happened to momma, grandma, great- grandma, or daddy, granddaddy, great-granddaddy it doesn't mean it has to be your story too.*

While this union produced irreversible changes in the two of them, there was also a new life that was factored into the equation, Krystal Denise Carr. One who inherited their iniquities… and so goes the case of two miseducated and unprepared teenagers faced with the burden of "being parents-to-soon" because they chose to act on "feelings" 🎶 "listen to my heart go dah, dah Boo'd up" (sang Ella Mai). Consequently, their twisted misconception of identity, the added pressures of parental responsibility, and their under-established relationship led to a whirlwind of rejection(s); rejection of the purpose-driven relationships, rejection of authentic love, and even rejection of a better life.

OPENING STATEMENT. Greetings ladies and gentlemen of the jury. My name is Krystal Denise Carr, I am representing myself in this civil suit. I am here today because certain safety laws that were meant to protect everyone, concerning sexual immorality and fornication, were broken. Let me tell you what happened…

On a cool fall day, December 3, 1977, a 6 lb. 12 oz. baby girl was born. I was the result of an unsanctioned union of two teenagers experimenting with a faux pas love relationship. Most people would venture to say that I was "a mistake." I was initially denied by my father and eventually shunned by my mother. The evidence will show that at the very time of my birth there was an occurrence of death simultaneously. Outwardly… a beautiful, precious, helpless infant; and in sin my parents conceived me. There was nothing I could do to avoid my parental inheritance. I was severely injured, although I didn't have any visible signs of trauma… no bleeding, bruises, or pain. It was my birthright, and surely HE would lay the sins of the parents upon their children; even children in the third and fourth generations [Numbers 14:18].

I was broken, although I appeared whole. I was ill, but I appeared healthy. I was dead, yet ironically full of life.

I've had to close doors that I never opened, fight battles that I didn't initiate, and cast down things I never exalted. I've endured pain and I *still* endure it today.

Today, you will hear from me and other witnesses, who saw the manifestations of emotional instability, promiscuity, adultery, brokenness, insecurity, withdrawal, and co-dependence.

Some of you may not be familiar with the legal processes, so here is what will happen. You, the jurors [readers] will consider the facts of my case. The Judge will instruct you about the law. As the Judge will inform you, my burden of proof will lie in my ability to show repentance on behalf of myself and others before me. If these are the scales of justice, all I need is a slight tipping of the scales in my favor to show *the* burden of proof (grace). It has been stated that we overcome by the blood of the lamb and by the word of our testimony. However, our adversary argues that he has evidence that will disqualify my purpose. I will do my best to prove to you that even though I committed the transgressions I was *still* on course.

Your Honor, the people call their first witness REJECTION to the stand. Do you swear to tell the truth, the whole truth, and nothing but the truth so help you GOD? "I do." REJECTION, for the record would you please state your name and the nature of the relationship between you and the defendant - Ms. Carr.

My name is REJECTION- (failure to show due affection or concern) and my first encounter with the defendant was the day of her birth, December 3, 1977. As I recall, her father was not present upon her arrival. As a matter of fact, WE denied her even before that day. The love games that were played at that time, hoodwinked another young lady that he was involved with and she also carried OUR seed. *Her daddy* faced fatherhood from two different avenues in close proximity. "I am not the father" led me straight to Krystal Denise Carr. From the moment of *her daddy's* initial denial, I claimed her. So even though *daddy* was not present, I was there at birth to hold her, to rock her, to discomfort her, to tell her "I don't love you", "I don't want you", "I want to destroy you... And I will." At least I *thought* I could.

In all actuality I've had a longstanding relationship with quite a few members of her family, we go wayyyyy back [I probably have a relationship with someone in your family too…]. When the opportunity presented itself to take on a new lifeform, I was there to stake *my* claim. What I require for a new start is innocence, that's what I like. Purity, and what is purer than a child? Unless you have a trained eye there is no way to detect my presence, I was there at birth, how can you see what you don't even know exists. I waited for the perfect time to manifest, I couldn't lay dormant forever, I couldn't be a whisper anymore! So, for the next four decades, I led Krystal to verbal abuse, physical abuse, emotional abuse… you know, that faux pas love that she loved so much. That was all me, yeah, that was all me! I am easily mistaken for something or someone else all the time. I am who I am... but you don't recognize me, you cannot see me *because* I am within you. Thus, if you never see YOU, you'll NEVER see me. Don't look in the "mirror," I don't like soul searching.

After my seed was implanted, I searched and utilized environments, circumstances, and situations in order to thrive and grow. From past experiences, I've learned that Krystal [*was* incredibly fertile... truth be told my inception was never about her...

The generations before just couldn't get it right. There were so many people that came close, but I guess I was just too intense for them to overcome. I learned from their mistakes even when they didn't and found ways to remain in their lives even though they rejected REJECTION. They failed to learn my motives and study my vices to combat my subtle and cunning ways. They just kept feeding me, like a family pet. Their ignorance allowed me to enter, comfortably reside, and spread like wildfire throughout the generations. Is it my fault if they allowed me to stay so long? Wouldn't you remain where you grew, even if you were not "welcomed?" Six months establishes residency. Stupid is what stupid does, you ain't stupid Krystal, you know I "love" you. Your honor I have bared witness.

FLASHBACK [12-year-old Krissy]

    "ALL THAT I OWE YOU, TAKE KRISSY FOR IT!", that's what my momma said. This was the first dose of poison I swallowed like necessary medicine. Her words gave me heartburn, and I was the pardon for my mother's indiscretions. The rejection was familiar, strong, and an abnormally soothing drink that set the course of my life. "My name is Krystal and I am a faux pas love-aholic."

    I threw my head back, opened my mouth wide, and without hesitation swiftly ingested the seething, bitter words of another. As my facial expression contorted with disdain and disgust, the words of rejection slid down my throat again... burning my esophagus as I swallowed "it" settled not only in my stomach, but it nestled comfortably within me and caused continual discomfort...

Chapter 2
Looking for Love
Case No. 96-101600FL
(Pivotal Point #2 October 16, 1996)

PRETRIAL. A cute, trendy, somewhat athletic high school junior met a muscular, fashionable, athletic jock sophomore. Krissy and let's call him Jermaine or "Jay". A relationship that should have been strangely uncommon was ironically typical. Krissy wasn't really attracted to Jermaine from the start, but he was persistent. Every day in PE class he saw her on the bleachers, then he came and sat very close to her and immediately turned on the charm. Initially, she rejected all of his advances. She didn't give him the time of day. When he approached her with his flirtatious shenanigans, she rolled her eyes and turned the other way.

Until one day, he finally wore her down and they started "talking". Through phone conversation, Krissy grew quite fond of Jay. Not that he was superbly interesting, but he seemed to be genuinely interested in her. As teenagers, there were not many options for the dating arena outside of the football games at school, the movies, and the occasional dinner date at McDonald's. This "male attention" exceeded the quantity and quality of "love" she was accustomed to [Rejection, had kept her company consistently… he still was]. The "relationship" grew, and "feelings" erupted. Krissy and Jay decided to act on these feelings one day when they were home alone. They found themselves connecting with each other in a way they hadn't before. They consummated the relationship, they touched, they fondled, and now they were connected sexually. The grasp of their sexual escapade was stronger than they could have possibly imagined.

    The initial encounter must have been good to them because the occurrences became more and more frequent. It happened in each other's rooms, in the backseat of the car, on the back of the truck, an abandoned mobile home, and they even missed the first period of the school day to drop by a relative's house who had left for work. "Anytime and Anyplace" 🎶(sing Janet, Ms. Jackson if you nasty) became their motto. Soon, their "relationship" only revolved around their sexual encounters. They spent time together, but it wasn't meaningful. Everything they did together from *that* point led directly to sex.

Krissy became bored with their relationship… she wanted more. There was a prospective fellow that she kind of had a secret crush on and he felt the same way about her. He had gone into the military after high school and he notified her that he would return home for a visit during the holidays. Of course, he wanted to see Krissy while he was home, and she was not opposed to it. She just had to figure out how to see this fellow without Jay finding out. After all this "crush" had more to offer.

Krissy set up a date when she knew Jay would be out of dodge. The date went smoothly, and they creeped without interruption… "So I creep, yeah just keep it on the down low so nobody is supposed to know" 🎵 (sang TLC). Until… Jay decided to make a surprise visit to Krissy's house to find "crush" chilling on the sofa. Jay was so devastated that he angrily turned around and left. Krissy asked "crush" to leave and tried to handle the situation as gently as possible. Needless to say, it did not go over well. Jay's mother showed up to intervene on behalf of her beloved son. Once she got wind of what happened, her response to fending for her 16-year-old son was shocking, inappropriate, and offensive. She proceeded to get in Krissy's 16-year-old face and call her a "slut with a capital S". That's nothing to say to a 16-year-old when you are a middle-aged adult... right? Yet, it happened. Krissy accepted it and thought that somehow, she may have deserved that because she knew she had wronged Jay. Krissy felt badly that she had hurt his feelings. Consequently, after that night Jay was forbidden to talk to Krissy anymore. Yet, against his mother's wishes he called her anyway. Because of the hurt that she caused, Krissy shifted her focus from "crush" back to Jay.

By this time "crush" had returned back to his military quarters. She tried to reconcile her "relationship" with Jay...

their lusts claimed each other's affections once more. This time Jay had a plan that came with a disclaimer. "When we have sex again, you better be careful because my intentions are to get you pregnant." This statement somehow intrigued Krissy, as she took this as a proclamation of "love", she eventually yielded to his request. After all she was responsible for his broken heart…right?

OPENING STATEMENT. "Hello people of the jury. My name is Krissy. As you can see, I am speaking for myself in this civil suit. Before this case, I've been in something like this before. I am here today because some laws that were meant to protect people, that had to do with sexing people you're not married to, were broken. This is what happened…"

On October 16, 1995 when I was 17 years old, I gave birth to a 6 lb. 5 oz baby girl. Her name is Keke… "Keke, do you love me are we ridin' say you'll never ever leave from beside me cause I want ya and I need ya and I'm down for you always" 🎵(sang Drake). I love my daughter and I never viewed her as a mistake; however, I did not like the circumstances surrounding her birth. Initially her daddy tried to deny her, but ultimately, he was there, and his momma supported us financially.

    My life changed in ways I didn't think were possible once I had Keke. I *became* a mother! I was NOT ready. Part of me died… and I felt as if the wrong part of me lived. I am here to prove that two negatives really can make a positive… I'm not talking about math. Physically, my baby was beautiful, precious, and innocent; Spiritually and inherently, I knew my baby would suffer with the same things I did… because I suffered from the same things that my momma suffered from, that her momma suffered from, and her momma's momma suffered from… shoot, Keke could not escape it [I'm sorry baby for my transgressions, I didn't realize the magnitude of my decisions]. My baby was hurt badly even though the trauma wasn't evident initially. Fatefully, her future was set because of the things "WE" did *before* her… Sound familiar?

Your honor the courts have previously heard the testimony from former witness REJECTION, and we would like to use that testimony as evidence in this case. The people call their second witness PROMISCUITY to the stand. Do you swear to tell the truth, the whole truth, and nothing but the truth so help you God? "I do". PROMISCUITY, for the record would you please state your name and the nature of the relationship between you and the defendant. My name is PROMISCUITY- (having many transient sexual relations; demonstrating or implying an undiscriminating or unselective approach), and I met the defendant at the moment of her conception. You see, me and Lil Bubba [Krissy's daddy] go way back, we've been pimpin' since pimpin' was pimpin'… "Papa was a rolling stone, wherever he laid his hat was his home" 🎵🎵(sang Temptations). We got Krissy's momma pregnant at the same time ol' girl cross town was pregnant… I don't discriminate. MY purpose is to multiply and divide. Not just becoming one but becoming many. Fruitful and multiplying is what I believe the direction is. Unfortunately, the misfortune was that the corruptible thing was over developing at a rapid rate. Rapid reproduction became my modus operandi (mode of operation). Baby Momma and Baby Daddy were already in my grasp. You should have seen the way I made them carry on in lust. It was so entertaining, it was definitely a Netflix and chill type of setup. The way that they just freely gave themselves to other people not knowing that every connection they made took a chip off the old block. Ignorant to the fact that each encounter led to a deficit that ultimately left them in ruins and remaining clueless in their identity and purpose. The "love them and leave them" game was real. The body count assigned to each of them was ridiculous, I think even I lost count. They carried so many people around with them that it was nearly impossible to sift through all the fragmented pieces to find themselves. They couldn't shake me even when they tried. Because of their appetite for "love" that left them depleted and purposely unsatisfied, they continued to feed on me attempting to satisfy a longing in their soul they believed could be gratified through sex. It's a shame they never found the real remedy for that. The same thing that I did to Big Momma and Big Poppa is the same thing that I did to Krissy. In her quest for "love" she searched in low places through the lenses of rejection and lust. Any guy that was *physically* appealing, or seemingly interested enough in *her simply* whispered bitter nothings disguised as sweet somethings in her ear became another body to add to the count of eternal and cancerous dissatisfaction. She was on a roll...literally, "between the sheets." The bait was taken when the "Jay and Crush" incident occurred... I knew from that day the game was on. One day Jay went away, and the girl did play. When she got tired of one dude, I persuaded her that it was time to move on to the next one. After a while her moral standards took a plunge and she was even down with a couple married dudes [sexual deviant she was...]. One dude in the front door, another dude out the back door. While one guy was in his bed, she cuddled with another guy on her living room floor.

I had Krissy so hooked, even the way she dressed changed. Nothing was left to the imagination, she just let it all hang out. "Promiscuous girl wherever you are, I'm all alone and it's you that I want. Promiscuous girl you teasing me, you know what I want and you got what I need." 🎶 (sang Nelly Furtado). I had her, boy did I have her ...until one day my grip slipped. Your Honor, I have bared witness!

FLASHBACK. (14-year-old Krissy)

"BOY SHE GONNA BE FINE WHEN SHE GET OLDER", that's what the older guys would say in passing. As a younger teenager, older men were attracted to me and I'm sure it was for all the wrong reasons. However, in my young mind, I thought it was admirable to get attention from older guys. When I heard comments like these, I smiled with innocent flattery not knowing that these words were fertilizing corrupt seeds. They accepted the innocence of my smiles as an invitation or approval of some sort. Soon their words turned into advances. It was as if there was some strange pheromone that permeated and caused them to target and inevitably pursue me. What caused these older men to be attracted to someone much younger? Were they after my purity, my innocence? I surely wasn't offering it up, but it was as if they preyed for the perfect opportunity to creep in unaware... The voices of the men I encountered seemed to be soothing because it

filled a void that was reserved for my father to fill. He should have been the one showering me with affirmations of my beauty, intelligence, and worth. Instead his portion was filled with a sea of affliction causing troubled waters. Due to his disposition I could not properly align with my full potential because I was empty and dying of thirst...

A defiled "love" quenched my thirst. I drank from waters that were bitter, stagnant, and infectious all because I longed for the approving voice of my father... This constant longing rang loudly in the ears of the men that made advances, and they danced to the lustful and perverted melody of their desires... this had nothing to do with "how attractive" I was...

Chapter 3
Hooking Up with Lust

Case No. 98-100700FL;
Case No. 99-121200;
Case No. 00-080600
(Pivotal Points #3 October 07, 1998; December 12, 1999; August 06, 2000)

PRETRIAL. Thug life, hormonal teen boy meets innocent, sweet young girl at a softball game. We will call him Keith and of course, she's Krissy. "Hey Shorty, wassup with you," was a common line that preluded "the hookup." Grinning from ear to ear at the attention she received from an older guy, she entertained this guy lame excuse for courtship. Sadly, in this case Krissy fell for it… hook, line, and sinker. She yearned for Keith's attention. He wasn't even that cute, smart, or nice. It was the simple fact that he appeared to like her. Krissy was only fourteen at the time and Keith was seventeen. Not much of an age difference in general, but when you're a developing teenager with differences in upbringing and experiences… they were worlds apart. Keith and Krissy developed a "situationship." It was a form of something, but not love. It was basically just company.

Initially there wasn't any sex in the friendship/relationship. Sometimes a kiss, infrequent holding of hands, and occasional "dry-humping." Krissy was too young to go anywhere without an escort. At least that's how her grandmother felt. And there was no opportunity given for anything outside of that to happen. The combination of Keith's experiences and hormones got the best of him and he decided to pursue other relationships that were sexually beneficial. Eventually, the "situationship" between Keith and Krissy dissipated.

However, years later as Krissy was plagued by Promiscuity, they found their way back to each other and it was on! After Krissy had been through a few guys herself and had matching experiences with Keith, they now had somethings in common and they made sure to exercise that commonality often, "OOOhhh, ooh, ooh, ooh, I wanna sex you up" 🎵(sing it Color Me Badd). These encounters were strictly sexual, there was nothing else that these two had in common, just hookups and sex. Sex in the morning, sex in the afternoon, and sex in the evening. They satisfied their sexual urges like they satisfied their hunger for food and drink! Their sexual adventures did not develop any form of intimacy or worthy communication. It felt good until they got too careless and got caught. Yes, you guessed it Krissy, became pregnant. She almost had an abortion. She went as far as to go to the abortion clinic, they explained the entire process with graphic pictures and that was enough to change her mind.

OPENING STATEMENT. Ladies and gentlemen of the jury. I, Krystal Carr also known as "Krissy", appear before the courts representing myself again. I've frequented this scene before as there have been several offenses laid to my charge. I'm a habitual offender. Before the verdict is rendered on this case, I have committed a related transgression. The charges laid to my account would deem me to be a sexual deviant (or freak in layman's terms): Count 1- Lust; Count 2- Fornication; Count 3- Adultery; and Count 4-Lasciviousness. SEX was the case that *they* gave me! The cases on the docket to be addressed are as follows Case No. 98- 100700FL, Case No. 99-121200FL, and Case No. 00-080600FL concurrently.

On October 7, 1998, a man child was born. I was the tender age of 20 and now a mother of two. Keiton was the fruit of an explicit sexual encounter, "as we lay we should have thought about tomorrow and the price we had to pay" 🎵 (sing Shirley Murdock), but we didn't. There was no "love", it was strictly-dickly as the saying goes. Because this pregnancy was unplanned and unwanted *at the time*, Keiton was almost aborted. I was still so young, and I already had one baby. How could I manage two? The plan was that when my income tax money arrived that I would take a trip to the clinic to get rid of my "little problem" because I didn't know he was purposed... When I told Keith of my plans, he agreed that it was best for both of us.

So, I went to the abortion clinic. What I found out that day would be both educational and life-changing. The initial consultation in this particular clinic included counseling. They shared pertinent information about the procedure, then they recommended that I carefully considered everything we discussed. First, the counselor lady prayed with me. Then, she proceeded to explain the graphic, and horrific processes to me. There were pictures of a mangled fetus inside the uterus, then the remains of the unborn child were suctioned out. This heinous process caused scarring to the uterus and possible complications for future pregnancies.

After the counselor's explanation she prayed with me again and went through other options such as adoption. I knew that adoption was not an option that I would exercise. Ultimately, I decided to keep Keiton. It was a hard decision, but I chose to do the best that I could by this little precious boy of mine. Keith and I didn't have a relationship, so we fell off after a while. I went through eight months of pregnancy without him. Even though I was pregnant that did not dismiss my lustful appetite. In fact, it was heightened. However, there was a decrease in the number of partners, after all I was with child. Again, it was strictly sexual, and I was already pregnant, so I figured the worst had already happened.

Going into my ninth month of pregnancy I started to get lonely and I wanted my baby to know that he had a father, so I sought Keith out in hopes to develop some type of friendship for the sake of the baby. We tried to establish some type of arrangement from that point on. Needless to say, it wasn't much, but *to me* it was better than nothing. Keith and I tolerated each other, and sex was the main attraction between us. Aggression and sex became our lot in the marriage. We fought all the time, then had sex to assuage the tension between us. This sexual compensation gave us a couple minutes of pleasure and two babies.

It wasn't until Keith became ill that he started to look at life a little differently... momentarily. Keith suffered from intense abdominal pain and he had mass swelling on the side of his neck. He was later diagnosed with Hodgkin's Lymphoma. Keith decided that he wanted to get married during his illness. I married him because I would have felt guilty if something detrimental happened to him.

Case No. 99-121200FL... "I do, [take one]. We got married and it was the WORST mistake I ever made... Well, one of them. Myles Munroe says, "When a purpose of a thing is unknown or misunderstood, abuse is inevitable". This was a hard lesson to learn. Neither one of us knew the true purpose of marriage and thus we abused ourselves and subjected our children to our turmoil.

Then along came another beautiful bouncing baby boy, Dewayne; Case No. 00-080600FL. "Behold, I was brought forth in iniquity and in sin did my mother conceive me" (Psalm 51:5). The conception in sin took place when all precautions were taken to make sure that no seed was planted and yet seed was planted anyway. So now the sins of the father and the state of the mother collide and bring forth new life. Not only was this child born full of the sin that was passed down through the bloodline of his fathers, but he was also plagued with same struggles his mother fought (Rejection, Promiscuity, Low Self-esteem, Self-doubt, & Unworthiness, etc.)... Get the picture?

After months of birth control and sterilizing chemo treatments, we ended up pregnant again despite the incompatibility between us. Our relationship fell soon thereafter, and the fall was tremendous because we didn't have a solid foundation. It was established by sex and maintained through fear. It was the most tumultuous thing that I had ever went through at that point in my life. Our last encounter led to broken furniture, broken windows, a wounded son, and a vivid reality check. We were not meant to be together, but we tried to force something that was never meant to be.

Upon the break up there were exchanges of words that were made from Keith to Krissy. With the many cruel things that were exchanged the thing that stuck with Krissy was that no one will want you with three kids. But that wasn't the saddest part, the most disheartening thing was that I believed it.

Your honor the courts have previously heard testimony from former witnesses REJECTION and PROMISCUITY. We would like to use their testimonies as evidence in this case also. The people call their third witness LOW SELF-ESTEEM to the stand. Do you swear to tell the truth, the whole truth, and nothing but the truth so help you God? "I do". LOW SELF-ESTEEM, for the record would you please state your name and the nature of the relationship between you and the defendant.

My name is LOW SELF ESTEEM (LSE) - (lack of confidence, feeling poorly about oneself causing one to judge self to be inferior to others), and I met the defendant when she was on the swim team at Cooper Island. I was present in the seed of her father. Why do you think that he had so many women? It surely wasn't because he was the gift to women. It was me that caused him to have multiple partners because of how he felt about himself. He didn't know who he was, so he needed continuous validation from others. He was plagued by the poison in my stinger and because this plague spread by way of sexual transmission, he passed the LSE gene on to Krissy. Krissy was a boss at carrying the trait. I mean to look at her, you would think that she had it all together. She spent hours grooming herself to mask the lowliness that she felt. The better she looked, the worst she felt. What you saw is what you didn't get. She was picture perfect... "Oh you fancy, huh...Nails done, hair done, everything did (sang Drake); but behind the mask was this timid girl who knew nothing about herself and nothing about the world in which she existed. *That house* was the perfect dwelling place for me. Not only did I live in that house, but her door swung open so much that she unknowingly invited some other relatives in.

When I moved in, REJECTION had a room, PROMISCUITY had a suite, so I took the master bedroom. The people that she allowed to enter through her door also carried the poison of my sting. Game recognizes game is how I've heard it spoken. Most men often glorify "the game". Consequently, it's easier to claim player status than to face the form that becomes you. I affected them so deeply that they would work tirelessly thinking of ways to overcompensate what they underestimated... *themselves*.

It's a shame that the guy I worked for knew more about them than they knew of themselves. Mr. D'vil (my boss) says that my job was to create a diversion to keep them from finding out *who* they are. I must say that I did my job and I did it well. As I was assigned, I got a report of Krissy and created opposing situations that made what could have been good fruit appear bad. The report stated that she was created in HIS image and in HIS likeness, but I made her feel like dirt. She was created to be fruitful and to multiply, but I caused her bones to be ridden with rottenness and created division. She was created to replenish and subdue the earth, but I caused her to be diminished and enslaved. She was created to have dominion over the fish of the sea, over the fowl of the air, and over every living thing that creeps on the earth, but I caused the fish to swallow her up, the fowl to pick at her flesh, and caused her to be a creeper in the earth. She was clothed in glory, but I stripped her naked. I did this so subtly, and because of her reprobate mentality she dressed *it* up in the finest clothes, got the fiercest hairstyle; rocked the latest kicks, bought the biggest earrings, and stepped in the highest heels… but internally - she rotted, *almost to her core.*

That house (Krissy) *was* my happy place, until… one day she read her own report and **believed** it, then I was left homeless. Your honor, I have bared witness.

FLASHBACK. (22-year-old Krissy)

"NOBODY'S GOING TO WANT YOU WITH THREE KIDS", were the words that he belted out when he knew I was leaving him. Was this a mind game to make me stay?

Was it true? There it goes again, that intoxicating drink that I am so accustomed to. Another day, another dose. "Bottoms up, bottoms up, let me fill your cup," 🎵 sang Tre Songz. Somewhere along the way I believed that I would have to settle for a piece of a man because no decent man was going to want a woman with a readymade family. I thought one child is bad enough, but I had three children. I believed I was out of the race before it began. I inadvertently lowered my standards to match the level of my self-esteem. Any man that seemed to have an inkling of interest in me and liked my kids was good enough for me to settle for. Who cares if there was something about him that I didn't like? I made myself like him and overrode the feeling in my heart that told me "you can do better than that", I didn't believe it, so I settled. I settled not once, not twice, but many times.

Chapter 4
Trying to *Right* My *Wrongs*
Case No. 06-122200FL
(Pivotal Point #4 December 22, 2006)

PRETRIAL. "Do you take this "man" to be your lawfully wedded husband?" I do... take two. "OOPS, I did it again" (sing Britney Spears). Older, "God-fearing" gentleman meets broken, lonely young woman. His name, "Lamont", and her name, Krystal. They met at a very crucial period in her life. She was going through major life transitions and her circumstances were messy. Krystal had just been reintroduced to Jesus and it was evident that this newly re-established relationship really shook things up.

At this point it was very difficult to tell whether it was for the good or for the bad.... Because there was a streamline of unfortunate events that occurred. She had just broken up with her boyfriend, wrecked her car, and lost her job all within the span of six months. In her quest for more knowledge and understanding, Krystal attended more church services, bible studies, and prayer meetings. She developed an insatiable appetite for the Word of God like never before and every chance she got she feasted and drank on it.

One fateful night during prayer meeting at a friend's house, Krystal encountered an older gentleman who led prayer and seemed to call the kingdom of heaven down into that place. His *perceived* love for God was extremely attractive to her. With all the turmoil that had been going on in her life, is this what she had been waiting and praying for, right? Was this a man after God's heart? Could he be trusted with Krystal's heart? *Only* God knew but she didn't think to *ask* Him.

Through mutual friends, Lamont expressed an interest in Krystal. Now, the "friends" had to make this "love" connection happen. Although, Krystal's physical attraction to Lamont was nonexistent, it was something about the way that he called on Jesus that lured her attention. However, she learned the hard-way (retrospectively) that not everyone one who calls on the Lord, is *close* to His heart.

Anyway, Krystal fell under the pressure and gave into Lamont's pursuit. After all they both loved Jesus, that was reason *enough,* right or wrong? They both wanted to walk according to His will and His way, right? They both had a vested interest in their relationship with The Father, right? However, things *are not always* what they appear to be. Krystal and Lamont "dated" for whopping two weeks, that's right, TWO WEEKS before they decided to follow "God's plan" for their life and marry instead of burn. Looking back, I can attest that if she had "One Wish" like Ray J, she would have wished that she had "Let it Burn", like Usher.

They were married by the same friends that were responsible for making the "godly-love connection." Since, she thought that she was incapable of choosing a suitable mate for herself, she left that in the hands of others who *were* possibly better decision-makers for her life [sounds ludicrous, I know!]. Big mistake. Surrounded by a few family members and friends they held a mini ceremony at their friends' house, where the wife, being a notary republic, officiated and approved the licensure. The moment after the "I dos" were exchanged, Krystal's stomach was in knots. She felt that she had made another huge mistake and didn't know how to get out of it. The next few days were a fog. She moped around trying to figure out how to get out of this *shit* that she had "married" into [sometimes you just have to call things how they are].

One day Lamont retorted, "I know you don't love me, so we don't have to turn in those licenses for the record if you don't want to." There was her escape, served on a silver platter. But guess what, like a fool she didn't take it. She felt sorry for him and thought about all the people who had witnessed their union, how would she explain the demise of their marriage before it even begin? Oh well... she thought "I'll just make the best of this," but it got the best of her in the end.

The relationship was okay in the beginning. He was a nice guy, super attentive, and he loved her kids. Lamont went on to become an ordained minister and was permitted to preach the gospel in churches on different occasions. They attended church every Sunday, did Bible studies together, and traveled as a family. There was just one thing missing.... LOVE, not even the faux pas love was present. During the course of this relationship, Krystal became lonelier and disdainfully disgusted with *Lamont, the marriage, and her life*. The "God fearing" husband, turned out to be a "Satan serving" crackhead. There were times when he left their house and went on drug-binges for several days. Then after being in the "crackhouse," he returned home, cleaned up, and prepared to preach *his* Sunday Sermon.

    Consequently, after the numerous disappearing acts Krystal searched for him, cleaned him up, and believed that he would get it together... she could not handle the theatrics that he put on from the pulpit on Sundays after being high and out of his mind all week. "Talking out your neck saying you a Christian... Now, that was the sin that did Jezebel in, how you gonna win when you ain't right within?" 🎶 (sang

Lauryn) . It's sad to say that she put up with a lot from this man that she never loved from the start… unemployment, stealing money, but the one thing that she could not and would not remain for was him making a mockery of GOD. Consequently, after less than a year of marriage it ended abruptly [and expectedly - ain't nobody got time for that!] … 🎵 "Another one bites the dust" (sang Queen).

OPENING STATEMENT. Greetings once again. This is not a case of who done it. The person who is charged with the aforementioned crimes stands before you. I am the DEFENDANT, Krystal Denise Carr Galloway Wheeler. The people inadvertently affected by my warped state of mind are my three innocent children; Keyana, Keiton, and Dewayne. I love them, and they are the greatest blessings in my life. I have spent my life trying my best to protect them; yet in all my efforts I unintentionally inflicted pain and harm upon them in my ignorance. Too frequently, my pursuit of happiness placed them second. In numerous attempts to make their lives better I made it worst. Thinking the authenticity of a mother's love alone was not enough for them, I sought for more, not realizing that I neglected and stunted their growth with supplemental aids. As I searched for a man to "complete" me and the idea of family, I left the THREE to find "*The One.*" Ladies and gentlemen of the jury, the question has been posed "If a man has ninety-nine sheep and one of them goes astray, will he not leave the ninety-nine on the hills to go out and search for the one that is lost? If he finds it, he will rejoice more for that one that was lost than for the ninety-nine that didn't go astray" (Matthew 18:12).

Unfortunately, I took the Word and twisted it to "fit" my situation instead of taking it as is, and allow it to "fix" my situation. It was never my duty *to leave to find anything.* The WORD says **HE FINDS**. It is also stated that "He who finds a **WIFE** finds a good thing and obtains favor of the LORD" (Proverbs 18:22), not the other way around. *He goes out and searches for the one that is lost, not her.* Furthermore; it never notates whether he leaves the ninety-nine alone when he searches for the one, but I can almost guarantee that he didn't. In another excerpt it mentions that HE will never leave us nor forsake us, and if He did have to leave for any reason, HE will send THE COMFORTER (John 14:16). I've left and returned on many occasions, but since I was the one and only caregiver, there was no one to send in my stead. Therefore, in my efforts to find and bring home *"The One,"* I left them "ALONE." For this, I have the deepest regret. Your Honor, ladies and gentlemen of the jury… I throw myself at the mercy of the court in hopes that I be granted a pardon for my ignorance now that I have acknowledged and understand the error of my ways. Please, I fervently ask for your forgiveness.

Your honor the courts have heard and entered into evidence the previous testimonies of REJECTION, PROMISCUITY, and LOW-SELF ESTEEM. We now call the fourth and fifth witnesses to the stand, I say witnesses because this particular witness slightly differs from the rest. They happen to be conjoined twins- two entities that are physically connected to each other. The prosecution would like to call SELF-DOUBT and UNWORTHINESS to the stand. Because of their uniqueness we will hear testimony from the two of them as one… but they will answer simultaneously. SELF- DOUBT and UNWORTHINESS, do you swear to tell the truth, the whole truth, and nothing but the truth so help you God? "We do". SELF-DOUBT and UNWORTHINESS, for the record would you please state your names and the nature of the relationship between you and the defendant.

My name is SELF-DOUBT (the lack of belief in the reliability of one's own motives, personality, thoughts, decisions, and abilities) and I am UNWORTHINESS (insufficient worth or value; undeserving, unworthy of love). We met Krystal in Eve's Garden (the womb of her mother). It was us that intercepted the seeds of joy, fulfillment, and freedom… we produced misery, emptiness, and imprisonment. We are the corrupt soil that caused the fruit to appear appetizing, desirable, and consumable but in the end, it brought forth death and disease. Since she already dealt with REJECTION, it was easy for us to infiltrate the garden.

When she was a young girl, she was very smart, but we made her think otherwise. During her school age years, she usually knew the answers to the many questions that the teacher asked, but she never raised her hand to answer. Krystal always waited for another student to give the answer that she already knew and then she nodded her head in agreement. WE paralyzed her educational interaction to disprove her intelligence and the progression thereof eventually led to the immobilization of her entire being. Although she knew things, she remained silent because WE were rooted *within* her.

The trend began as a child, but as she matured, so did we. Like the black plague, we spread rapidly and aggressively attacked her at the very core of her being. Not only were we after Krystal, but we also planned to pursue everything, and everyone ***ATTACHED*** to her. Our soil was utterly corrupted. We caused her to be bound by the mental and emotional shackles of shame, pain, and despair. The things she hated, were the very things she attracted, loved, and nurtured. Instead of love she chose "faux pas love", instead of joy she chose sorrow, instead of peace she chose chaos, instead of patience she chose intolerance, instead of kindness she chose hostility, instead of goodness she chose indecency, instead of faithfulness she chose treachery, and instead of self-control she chose impulsive recklessness. To our benefit, she didn't plant these seeds, but Krystal *was* the perfect ground for *our* harvest, thus she inevitably reaped.

Until …. the foundations of the earth began to change and take on a different form. Now the seeds that we once intercepted began to reject and eject from the corrupt soil like an erupting volcano … and soon we were forced to leave our place of reproduction only to be left infertile and barren. We thought that our placement was secure, our production line was booming, but the grounds were now being irrigated differently and we could no longer thrive in that place… So, we left... "Hit the road Jack, and don't you come back no more... what you say? (Sang Ray Charles). Your honor, we have bared witness.

FLASHBACK (8-year-old Krissy)

"TAKE YOUR BOOKBAG AND WRAP IT AROUND YOUR TONGUE", were the words of my third-grade teacher who thought I was talking too much. Those words from a close stranger pierced my young little heart to the core. I didn't understand how I could invoke such an unpleasant reaction from someone simply by talking. Was I talking too much? Was I talking too loudly? Why is she so mad? ... I only asked my neighboring classmates for one of those green apple-flavored "now and later" candies that I loved so much. How could she say something like that to me? I didn't understand.

I decided it was best to be quiet from then on, especially since I didn't know what mistake I made or how to correct it. It was never communicated to me in a way I could understand? My young mind could not comprehend the level of hostility that she presented that day. Or was I just so obnoxious and oblivious that she could clearly see my worthlessness when I couldn't.

At the tender age of eight, I wasn't equipped to handle that large of a dose of toxicity. So, I ingested what I could of the frothy formula and spit up the rest. The spit up came in the form of a letter addressed to the teacher. Eight-year-old Krissy explained to her that she was going to go to HELL if she continued to be mean for no reason. This was her way of rejecting the excessive quantities then, but as the years progressed, she became somewhat conditioned to the poison and it became easier to swallow despite its potency.

Chapter 5
Loving Mr. Wrong, *Again*
Case No. 09-072700
(Pivotal Point #5 July 27, 2009)

PRETRIAL. "I Krystal, take you, Lamar to be my awfully, I mean, lawfully wedded husband, to have and to hold, from this day forward, for better, for worse, for richer, for poorer, in sickness and in health, to love and to cherish, till death do us part..." but *whose* death will cause us to part? I do... *take three*!

You have got to be kidding right? Is this happening again? How stupid can one person be in a lifetime? "What's not clicking up there? Do you ever think? I've been waiting while you were galivanting. DON'T LET THIS HAPPEN AGAIN! I don't have time for this, and I don't have time *for you* either." I stood there, quietly flabbergasted, embarrassed, and questionably afraid, not of him... but what I anticipated, I had been "here" before.

Apparently, life offers a plethora of opportunities to be stupid and it seemed that Krystal took advantage of every one of them. What makes this one any different from the rest?

Saved, sanctified, and Holy Ghost filled "pietist" meets tall, dark, and handsome "slickster". After months of being alone and soul searching, Krystal decided that she was "ready for love... why are you hiding from me? I'd quickly give my freedom to be held in your captivity" 🎵 (sang India Arie). This time *it* would be different... but did she pray and listen to specific instructions from God before committing to another king? She waited... yes. She prayed... yes. But did she listen to SPECIFIC instruction...the jury is still in deliberation on that matter.

Meeting place: Walmart. Meeting someone at Walmart, the home of Clearances, Rollbacks, and Big Savings should have been a clear indication that this was not the place to land a man! Apparently, he offered a discount that should have simply been thrown away. She should have studied the price tag that came along with him a little closer. From the beginning, it seemed all wrong but alright at the same time. Initially, Lamar was charming, attentive, and charismatic; however, he had a flip side. His personality switched like that of Dr. Jekyll and Mr. Hyde. When things operated outside of his ability to manage, his coping strategies were demeaning, inattentive, cruel, and abusive… verbally, mentally, emotionally, and physically.

Initial indication of conflict: "Why are you looking other niggas in their eyes?" "You tryin' to get their attention or something?" "Don't fuckin' disrespect me like that, I will cut the fuck up." Confused at the level of disrespect she experienced, Krystal attempted to plead her case, but the more she opposed his ridiculous accusations, the more his behavior escalated. Sadly, the confrontation ended with her being pushed over a small hedge and knocked to the ground. As she picked herself up and brushed herself off, she was met with what seemed to be sincere apologies and a contrite heart.

Lamar seemed to have felt so badly that he wanted to do whatever it took to make it up to Krystal. He took her on a date as a gesture to prove how apologetic he was.

While on the date, he offered his "most genuine" complete with tears and sniffles. Krystal was moved by these gestures as she accepted his perpetual lie.... *"this will never happen again"* and consoled him through the tears as she assured him that he was forgiven. Little did she know; this performance would be the first of many. Act one should have been the final curtain call, but unfortunately it was the beginning of a seemingly constant replay.

Although this relationship proved to be unhealthy on many levels, Krystal was determined to fight and make it work. She prayed, cried, and endured ...thinking that surely things would get better after a while. She loved him when he was good, and loved him even more when he was bad. She felt as if she was addicted to the pain and this pain challenged her to love *him* [instead of HIM] even the more. How was this possible? How could someone who is loved so much treat the one who loves them so badly? I suppose that's how Jesus felt as HE loved the world and the world hated HIM. How long would she endure and continue in this cycle of despair. One year? Two years? Three years?... Nope, NINE Years? Really??? Eye roll. Surely, she has more sense than that… or maybe she didn't. Maybe, that place called "Lala Land" was her dwelling place…

OPENING STATEMENT. Ladies and gentlemen of the jury. At this particular time, I don't think a greeting is necessary. You all know who I am, but in the event that your memory has failed you, allow me to offer a reminder. My name is Krystal Denise Carr Galloway Wheeler Thomas aka Krissy. By now, I know that I have exhausted you all with my many appearances and truthfully, I also am wearied with making appearances before you. Let's omit the formalities and cut to the chase…

There have been many charges laid to my account but this by far has outweighed them all. I've tried to be a good daughter, mother, wife, friend, and person. In each one of those relational areas I seemed to have fallen short at one time or another. My shortcomings have not only affected my life, but also the lives of those who share life with me. On occasions, I've been the exact opposite of what I was supposed to be while hiding my true identity behind a mask of what I thought was acceptable. I've been a liar, a cheater, an adulterer, a fornicator, a manipulator, a thief, along with many other things. Because of the relationships that developed with Rejection, Promiscuity, Low Self-esteem, Self-doubt, and Unworthiness my behavior manifested in various forms.

    It wasn't that I didn't know, it wasn't that I didn't recognize it, it was the "me" that I became accustomed to and I was comfortably uncomfortable with "me". As long as I could continue to hide, I embodied "fake it till I make it." Not only was I dealing with my own sinful nature, but also the sinful nature of those that were bonded to my soul, whether by transmission, omission, or commission. Paul said it best when he proclaimed "Oh wretched man that I am!

Who shall deliver me from this body of death?" (Romans 7:24). Character traits were passed on that didn't necessarily belong to me but were inherently mine and transferred inherently to my children. What did I overlook? Why did I ignore it? Why did I mask it? Why didn't I take the time to dissect it? ... BARE WITNESS.

Your honor the courts have heard and entered into evidence the previous testimonies of former witnesses REJECTION, PROMISCUITY, LOW-SELF ESTEEM, SELF-DOUBT, and UNWORTHINESS. We now call the sixth witness to the stand. The prosecution calls POVERTY to the stand. POVERTY do you swear to tell the truth, the whole truth, and nothing but the truth so help you God? "I do."

POVERTY for the record would you please state your name and the nature of the relationship between you and the defendant. My name is POVERTY (the state of being extremely poor, inferior in quality or insufficient in amount). I met Krystal through mutual friends

REJECTION, PROMISCUITY, LOW-SELF ESTEEM, SELF-DOUBT, and UNWORTHINESS. They were the conduits that led me right to her. After they had their way with her, I was the one who was responsible for her destitution. She *spent* so much time trying to rid herself from the plagues of our friends that she carelessly invited me, adding to her destruction instead of making room for renovation.

The party of six became the party of seven, the perfect environment for calamity. While everyone served their purpose, I entered to extract any inkling of life that was left. Every time she had a moment to breathe, I choked her out again. This was a game of Mortal Kombat, and my duty was to "Finish her!" I must say, she is a resilient one. She definitely went round for round, but in the end she was no match for me. I was the confiscator of her peace, joy, humility, love, and almost her sanity.

Until one day... Krystal realized her strength was insufficient and she stopped fighting her own battles.

Someone stepped in to fight for her. It was then that I noticed the things that I thought I retrieved and secured from her were returned and there was nothing I could do to stop it.

Your honor, I have bared witness...

FLASHBACK (Adult Krystal)
"YOU ARE NOT A WIFE, YOU ARE A WASTE OF TIME". Words of nullification, that regularly solidified my place with him. When things didn't go as he wanted, when he wanted... this was the drink that was best served COLD. Somehow, he was satisfied watching as I chewed and swallowed these bitter words like small chips of ice. He watched in anticipation and felt a sense of empowerment as he observed the goosebumps raising visibly on my body from the callous chill of his venomous words.

FLASHFORWARD
"YOU ARE THE BEST THING I'VE EVER HAD." Words that commonly followed an occurrence of disrespect and rage. He played dual roles of the villain and the hero within the same episode. Exhaling he hated me, and inhaling he loved me simultaneously. He seemed so convincing when he made these statements. When he hated me, I believed him but when he "loved me," I believed that too! The conflict remained because I didn't know what was true... the "love" or the hate? So, I trusted what I hoped for instead of what was proven.

FLASHBACK
"YEAH, GO AHEAD AND PUT MAKEUP ON, YOU NEED IT". Not only did he use his insecurities to attack my inner beauty, but also to diminish my outer confidence. These words were so aggressive and destructive as they spewed out of his mouth like flood waters from a failed dam. Too much to ingest at times, these waters filled every available space in my bowels, then my lungs, and finally caused me to fall unconscious as I drowned in despair.

FLASHBACK
"YOU ARE SO BEAUTIFUL TO ME". The mouth to mouth resuscitation that brings me back to life after a near fatality. He loves me, he loves me not, he loves me, he loves me not was the silly little game we played as the pendulum swung in the balance between life and death. I willingly participated in this dangerous game. WHY did I cleave to something that I abhorred, despised, loathed, simply and utterly hated? I had developed and acquired a taste for the poison… because I believed that small doses presented as vaccinations were temporarily soothing, without realizing the latent and inevitable outcome from drinking his poison… DEATH. Death of a bachelor to the bride led to death by association. DEATH of her self-esteem, her confidence, her emotional stability, her identity, her security, her peace of mind, her relationship with her children, and ultimately her seed.

CHAPTER 6
Death Was the Necessary Part
Case No.18-042800
(Pivotal Point #6 April 28, 2018)

PRETRIAL. "Until death do us part". Enough was finally enough. It was a shame that it took her staring DEATH in the face for her to realize that LIFE was worth far more than what she had experienced the past nine years or forty for that matter. She wished that she had come to this realization long before now. Long before her transgressions, her iniquities, her struggles, her insecurities, and other tendencies that were inherently adopted and adapted… caught up with her. "How can I make sure that I fool everyone, gonna wear a *dress* and *heels* and put on my happiest face and it's far too deep to show you this wound. No, it won't heal any time soon. Nobody knows what I'm going through… I'm dying inside. Who knows what I'm thinking? What I'm trying to hide? Yeah, I'm dying all night, I'm breathing but I can't feel life. I'm smiling but dying inside" 🎶 ... (sing Gary Barlow).

IF it were only her dying, she could handle the pain. The feeling of touch and go as she was choked seemed sadistically pleasurable. So much time was spent in and out of consciousness, she didn't realize how much of an effect it had on the ones that were closest to her... her children. They watched her while no one watched them. Although her babies had been physically detached from her umbilical cord, they were yet connected and dependent on the very life-giving nutrients of her care, attention, love, affirmation, and support.

The processes of labor and delivery were far from over and whatever she experienced they experienced as well. Asphyxiation, lack of oxygen, through her led to their disabilities and developmental delays. Their inability to breathe made their condition much more critical than hers because of the limited capacity to withstand multiple traumatic episodes.

Her youngest child, Dewayne, was the most sensitive and most susceptible to her condition… as she was *his* lifeline. They were one in the same as he was the most dependent on firm leadership and guidance because of the gifting that was laid to his charge. The habitual addiction to toxoids and their joyful effects inseparably passed through her system intravenously and into his. Continuous exposure to these contaminants eventually led to the lethal injection that caused the cessation of his heart. And on the day his heart stopped beating… so did hers.

OPENING STATEMENT. Ladies and gentlemen of the jury. It's me. I have no name, no identity, no existence, no thought... I am conscious of nothing. Here I stand, defeated, destitute, and bereaved. "How can I make sure I'm invisible? I find just a simple phrase that may say it all. Cause it's far too soon and not the right time for what my eyes have seen. "How can I make sure no one worries for me? because I don't need a helping hand, and don't want sympathy. I don't know what I need! What you can't see, it feels so broke that I can't see how I will cope. I'm dying inside" 🎶 (sang tearfully Gary Barlow).

So, ladies and gentlemen of the jury, allow the outside to mirror what has already materialized on the inside and sentence me to death. For I have fallen prey to the subtlety of the serpent, and he beguiled me to eat from the tree of knowledge of good and evil. The tree appeared to be good for food in that it was pleasant to the eye, so I took and ate of the fruit that was forbidden. My eyes were opened, and I saw that I was *naked*. I tried my best to construct a cover up. I did it with hair, makeup, fancy clothes, and shoes but nothing sufficed. The voice that walked through my garden continuously reminded me of where I stood... *naked* and *afraid*. Hostility dwelled between him and me, and between my seed and his seed. Great sorrow was multiplied unto me and in sorrow I brought forth children; and my desire was unto my husband, and he ruled over me (Genesis 3). This statement serves as my confession... taking the stand is not warranted, I **BARE WITNESS** even from this place, for I am guilty as charged.

Your honor the courts have heard and entered into evidence the previous testimonies of former witnesses REJECTION, PROMISCUITY, LOW-SELF ESTEEM, SELF-DOUBT, UNWORTHINESS, and POVERTY. We now call the seventh and final witness to the stand. The prosecution calls DEATH... DEATH do you swear to tell the truth, the whole truth, and nothing but the truth so help you God? "I do".

DEATH for the record would you please state your name and the nature of the relationship between you and the defendant. My name is DEATH (the end of life, the total and permanent cessation of all vital functions). I existed with her, beside her before time was time. At the pinnacle of her father's mountain, she leaped into the multiplying flowing rivers of *life* and there I was, lurking in the shadows, lying dormant until the perfect opportunity presented itself. On a cool Autumn's day, December 3, 1977 at 11:53 a.m., I stood tall and proud as my moment had finally arrived. A beautiful baby girl weighing six pounds, twelve ounces tasted the bitter sweet dose of the synchrony of *life* and DEATH in just one breath. Woven into the very fibers of *life*, there I was. We dwelt together in perfect harmony like the yin and the yang. "Everything I did, he did, it's like we came in pairs, everywhere I went, he went, like he was always there, and he was too! 🎶 (sang your song Kei… but who's your Brother's Keeper now?).

Life is my fraternal twin. We look nothing alike, yet we are birthed from the same womb. Every day is a battle with him as he fights to begin and continue, and I fight to cease and desist. We have both wandered through the wilderness with the person formerly known as Krystal, which I will call her "Doe… Jane Doe." There have been many battles in the wilderness with "Jane D", but *Life* seemed to have lucked out and won most of them. However, this last battle was a doozy… "I had to turn into a beast and now I'm going beast mode" 🎶(sang Kei and One Way J… I definitely caused a hell of a storm for you niggas to go through). "I came through like a wrecking ball… all I wanted was to break your walls… and yeah I wrecked you" 🎶(scream that thang Miley Cyrus). This battle was epic. All the battles that were lost before when it appeared that *Life* won the heavyweight title, I came in and claimed it with a vengeance. "I'm taking over, I have the truth… this is the mission to see it through… you're just another part of me, hee hee 🎶 (sang Michael Jackson).

    This "Doe-hoe" was too damn cocky and resilient for me, so when I saw her hanging on to *"Dear Life,"* I knew something big had to go down to loosen her grip. Then BAM!! Got 'em! Now, "I'm living my best *life*… ain't going back and forth with you niggas!" 🎶 (spit it Lil' Duval) …but got-damn, I put that little nigga on his back and his punk ass momma too! Smile bitch - smile bitch… smile!

Man, if there has ever been a royal f.u.c.k (flabbergasted & utterly cold kocked) I must say, on that day... I handed her one on a filthy-platter! I had multiple orgasms off that piece, emotionally, physically, and spiritually. This one hit kept me on cloud nine "oo-chie wally wally, oo-chie bang bang...he really really tried to hurt me, he really really turned me out, he really really made me scream and shout... oo-chie wally wally, oo-chie bang bang" 🎶 (sang Nas and Braveheart).

"Emotions make you cry sometime...Emotions make you sad sometimes" 🎶 (sang H-town). Hell, I had her crying all the time. Sit down, cry; stand up, cry; pass out, cry; wake up, cry; faded, cry; faded, cry 🎶 (thanks Kendrick Lamar for letting *her* borrow your swimming pool full of liquor to dive in). Her emotions were all over the place. I emptied her out until there was nothing left but a shell of who she was... once upon a dream. When *life* left the premises, there was a huge vacancy. The spot was pretty clean too, it was all swept and garnished and shit. When I saw this, I knew that it was time to get things poppin'. Some of my homies that were previously kicked out, I called them up and invited them back in. You know REJECTION and PROMISCUITY and LOW SELF ESTEEM and SELF DOUBT, UNWORTHINESS and POVERTY and Donner and Blitzen, but do you recall the most villainous M.F'er of all?.... 🎶 (thanks for the tunes Rudolph). "Muh" to the damn D.E.A.T.H the black faced hoodrat (I COME FOR EVERYBODY… AND USUALLY WITHOUT RESURRECTION).

When I came in, I brought seven others with me, we were going to make sure that there wouldn't be a "Still I rise" Maya Angelou moment for her. My boys showed up and showed out and we partied all the time, partied all the time, partied all the time 🎵 (sang Eddie Murphy). Soon that house was beaten beyond recognition.

There were holes in the roof, broken windows, doors hanging off the hinges, ripped up flooring, mildewed walls, and debris everywhere. That old building begin to lean. It would take nothing for this entire structure to topple over, so to finish what we started we clogged all portals and flooded the place. After a while the house was completely covered by water, like the earth in the days of Noah, but there was no boat to save a single soul.

Everything that was attached to this house went under. Every seed, every sacrifice, every tithe, every prayer, every praise, every word of worship with one accord, everything including her hallelujah belonged to me. DEATH is my name and putting an end to *life* is my game. I am the last enemy and King Kong ain't got nothing on me… GOODNIGHT DEWAYNE … GOOD EVENING "JANE DOE"… GOOD AFTERNOON KEITON…

GOOD MOURNING KEYANA… GOOD DAWNING HAYDEN. It's getting late, why you gotta be here? Beside me. Watching, needing, wanting me…I'm afraid, (Don't Be), I'm afraid, (Don't Be) I'm so scared that you'll hurt me, **twice** 🎵 (Krystal sings in her Floetry voice)… Your honor I have bared witness.

FLASHBACK (APRIL 28, 2018)

"WHERE IS DEWAYNE?" Frantically escaped from my nauseated insides as I searched the house for my baby-boy. I looked towards the front door and discovered it was unlocked, "Oh, he must have gone for a walk," I said to myself in as I tried to settle my nerves. I flung open the front door and looked to my right, out into the street in expectation to find my Dewayne returning home from a usual early morning walk to clear his mind… but that wasn't the case. So, I inhaled a deep breath as prepared to yell out his name, but I slowly turned to my left and saw him lying on the ground. Relieved I thought, "Why is this boy sleeping outside," as I shook my head. Suddenly, I focused in on an object protruding from his chest. My mouth dropped open, my soul seemingly left my body, and I was numb, life-less, and cold … I was a mirror image of what stared me in my face… DEATH.
"NO, NO, NO, NO, NO" were the only words that escaped the paralysis of my being. I just knew I had I died with him…

emotionally, spiritually, physically… BECAUSE THIS FOR DAMN SURE was not figuratively.

FLASHFORWARD

*Never in a million years did I think SUICIDAL DEATH would be the BIG JOKER used against me in the game of LIFE. This game sucks and I don't want to play it anymore. I fold. Here I am, a child of the MOST-HIGH GOD, doing everything I know to do, yet this is my lot… go figure. Hey Job, I heard you say, "Thou you slay me yet will I trust you" HOW???? And WHY in the HELL would you or could you trust after all the SHIT you've been through? God specifically handed you to SATAN and you still trust HIM? Hey David, I heard you singing "the LORD is my SHEPHERD and I will not lack anything." You also said in that same song that death was just a shadow. Then, what the F#CK is this DAVID. This for damn sure looks like LACK and DEATH at the same damn time… this AINT a shadow! I wanna know how you came to **this** conclusion. Solomon, can I holla at you for a minute? You said that DEATH and LIFE were in the power of my tongue. Well, I definitely didn't speak any of THIS! I spoke LIFE, but DEATH answered. Did you and the Heavenly host look at me and laugh? The LAST, but also the FIRST, my brother from another mother, JESUS. Now, YOU perform miracles and everything. You SAID we would do greater works than you did and what not. Water was turned into wine, the lame walked, the deaf spoke, the blind received sight, you even told Lazarus to get his DEAD ass up, and he did! Why didn't it work for me? I believed, I fasted, I prayed… but it*

DIDN'T work. Aren't you SUPPOSED to be my friend... WHY, "why'd you do the things you did, knowing that I love you so? Tell me whyyyyyyyyyyyyyyy?" (sang Jagged Edge).

FORESHADOW

JOB: Krystal, I did not charge God foolishly. The adversary pointed out my flaws and was permitted to lay hold of what was holding me. FEAR. As long as fear was the only driving force that caused me to pray, I could not be who GOD purposed me to be. I couldn't be upright and shun evil because I was afraid of it, so I prayed fearfully (not fervently) prayers to ward off the thing that I was too afraid to confront. Unfortunately, everything that was attached to my fear-based prayer died when it died in me, because I was the father who begot this and that. So, because I continued to trust HIM even in THE refining moment(s) I was no longer driven or defined by FEAR. GOD restored to me "a double portion" of everything that I **thought** *was lost. My latter end was greater than my beginning and HE will do the same for you. Keep trusting! (Job 42:12)*

DAVID: Krystal, the LORD is my SHEPHERD and HE is **yours** *too. (Psalm 23:1) The steps of a good man are ordered by the LORD (Psalm 37:23). HIS plans are not to harm you only to prosper you and bring you to an expected end (Jeremiah 29:11) Not an end that YOU expect, but the end that HE has in mind. Do you remember, when you exchanged your will for HIS? Well, did you read the fine print. What you see is temporary, but what you cannot see is eternal and that which you cannot see is more real than that which you can see (2 Corinthians 4:18) DEATH is indeed a shadow, but ONLY when* **light** *is* *present. For when there is an opaque object that obstructs the rays of light in a particular area it reflects a partial darkness. DEATH is but an obscured reflection of LIFE. Except a grain of wheat fall into the ground and die, it abideth alone: but if it die, it bringeth forth much fruit (John 12:24). GOD will use the foolish things to confound or confuse the wise (1 Corinthians 1:27). The foolishness of God is wiser than our wisest (1 Corinthians 1:25). The very thing that he allows and uses to develop us is the very thing that makes us question "are you the Christ or shall we look for another" (Matthew 11:3). Get ready to lie down, or rest in the pastures of prosperity, for the time is now that your table is being prepared (Psalm 23: 2). Keep enduring!*

THE FATHER, THE SON, and THE HOLY SPIRIT for these three are ONE: I AM THAT I AM. I AM NOT a man that I should lie, nor the son of man that I should repent. For all the promises of GOD in HIM are yea, and in HIM, A-men' unto the glory of GOD by us…

*Krystal, my beloved daughter, sister, and mother… to everything there is a season. Death and Life are indeed in the power of the tongue, did you ever think that maybe it wasn't your tongue that spoke death? Take a moment to examine yourself to see if you are in the faith. Greater works you shall do if you don't get weary in doing well, for in due season you will reap the harvest if you don't faint. I have prayed for you, in groanings that cannot be uttered, I have prayed that your faith **fails not** in your day of trouble. I am the friend that remains closer than a brother, the life of men, the word of the Almighty GOD. I am he that **lives** and **was** dead; and behold, I am alive forever more and I have the keys* *of hell and DEATH, so don't let his shadows deceive you, I am not mocked and the great work that has begun in you I am **faithful** to perform it. Keep the Faith! This IS NOT being done TO you… but FOR YOU and MY Glory!*

CHAPTER 7
Life after *Death*

CLOSING ARGUMENTS. Life. What does it all mean? He was asked this specific question. His initial response was, "I've never thought about it before". I suppose that this is one of the questions that should have been asked during the dating (data/ collecting information) phase. That initial response would have told me everything I needed to know or not know about him. After much thought, he finally constructed a "spiritually correct" answer that he thought would earn him applause or kudos. "It means Godly purpose to make the world a better place", he said. But how have you contributed to your Godly purpose at this point in your life, I asked? No answer... Next Question. What does death mean to you? A plain and simple, "the end" was his response without thought or hesitation. This was an indication that death was the more prominent thing in his life. Unfortunately, at that time, I didn't take the initiative to ask those deep questions and to discern his answers. No fault of his own, he was just being who he was and doing what he knew. I asked for a king; even when I was warned of all the behavior of the king, God took heed to my voice and gave me exactly what I asked for (1 Samuel 8-11). It was my own shallow and wishful thinking that lead me down a destructive path. We were warned about these crooked paths, the ones broad and wide and traveled by many. Yet, we travel in this way by the droves. The Word reveals that "there is a way that seems right to a man, but its end is the way to death" (Proverbs 14:12). All of my *life*, to this point has seemed to be encompassed by *death* - a plain and simple "the end". I've followed the paths of rejection, promiscuity, low self-esteem, self- doubt, unworthiness, and poverty that have seemed right to me for so long that it appeared to be an impossible feat to amend my crooked paths. The more I did to try to straighten things out, the worst the situation became. "I tried to drink it away, I tried to put one in the air, I tried to dance it away, I tried to change it with my hair. I ran up my credit cards, thought a dress would make it better. I tried to work it away, but that just made me even sadder. I tried to keep myself busy, I ran around in circles, I think I made myself dizzy. I slept it away, I sexed it away, I read it away... But it did not go away, away, away" 🎶 🎶 (sang Solange, I agree with your concept of cranes in the sky). If it were solely my decision, then *DEATH*-"the end" would be definitive.

Within these forty-one years of life, I have died several deaths. Given six-million ways to die, I believe I have chosen not just one, but at least fifteen thousand of them; one for every day that I have lived. I have suffered the death of relationships, death of marriages, death of a mother-figure, death of self-esteem and self-worth, emotional death, spiritual death, and the worst of them all ... the death of a beloved child.

When life departed, death emerged. Death was frigid (cold), somber (dark), stagnant (still), ghastly (pale), and eerily silent and yet it moved, breathed, walked, and talked. How could this be? How was it possible that signs of *life* existed within this savage beast called Death? Was there such an uncanny resemblance between the two entities that it became impossible to distinguish one from the other? Or was my discernment and vision so skewed that I failed to recognize their obvious differences…?

The pretentious connection between the death of my last marriage, the death of my last child, and my own near-death experience caused an awakening in me like never before. It led me to search out the truth, while in my life crisis. Proverbs 18:21 tells us that "Life and Death is in the power of the tongue" and Matthew 12:34 implies that the mouth speaks what the heart is full of. With these truths in mind, I concluded that in my ignorance and desperation, I followed a way that *was right to me*, but the end result was *indeed* death. He was tall, dark, charming, and handsome, but he was also dead. His throat was an open grave; his tongue practiced deceit. The poison of vipers was on his lips, his mouth was full of cursing and of bitterness, his feet were swift to shed blood, destruction and misery followed him. The way of peace he did not know and there was no fear of God before his eyes (Romans 3:13-18). I should have known him by his fruit, yet I overlooked his present state and peered into his potential- (possible, as opposed to actual). With this, I submitted myself to his potential while bypassing the a-ffects, e-ffects, and defects of his actual... He was actually a liar, when I needed the truth; a fighter when I needed a lover; and a sinner when I needed a priest. Nothing I did was ever "good enough for him" [because I was NOT for him]. I spent/wasted a significant amount of time trying to exclaim, proclaim, and reclaim my love for him while neglecting others [but more importantly neglecting HIM]. All I really wanted was to be happy, find a love that's mine it would be so sweet 🎵(sang Mary J Blige). Amos 3:3 asks, "How can two walk together except they agree to?" The answer, they cannot. Do not be bound together with unbelievers; for what partnership does righteousness have with lawlessness? Or what fellowship has light and darkness? (2 Corinthians 6:14). If ever there were an appropriate answer to these questions, I believe the answers would be none. Unfortunately, I have had to learn some very hard lessons and it wasn't until I was faced with the most challenging situations when the answers to life's mysteries became *"Krystal"* clear.

It's been said that hindsight is 20/20; If I knew then, what I know now... things would be very different, is the cliché of choice in this story. I would have rescinded my request for a king and there wouldn't have been a voluntary execution (**marr/i/age- marr-** *dying a horrible death*; **I**- *to myse*l*f* ; **age-** *a period in time*) in which I found myself barebacked (naked and unashamed) to a maggot infested, decomposing corpse that caused poison to nearly consume my system which made me and those that were attached to me sicker and sicker as we slowly approached a painful and stench-filled death. I should have let the dead bury the dead, instead I chose the road much traveled and carelessly invited unwanted guests to dwell with us... *Lamar knew his wife and she unintentionally conceived and bore his seed of enmity while under submission, and they unconsciously ushered death into their midst and until death they did part.*

Ironically, with each death that was suffered, there was a discovery that therein lied the opportunity of *new life* dwelling within each one. What appeared to be a hopeless "*the end*" to some things was *not* as plain and simple as it seemed. Although, in and surrounded by death, there was something on the inside of me that wouldn't allow me to lie down and stay there... even when I wanted to. The sickness that was experienced was not unto death, but for the glory of God, that the Son of God might be glorified by it (John 11:4). "I do not want you to be unaware, brothers, of the hardships that I have had and that we will face in the provinces of the earth. I was under a burden far beyond my ability to endure, so that I despaired even of life. Indeed, I felt that I were under the sentence of death. But this happened that I might not rely on myself, but on God who raises the dead" (2

Corinthians 1:9). For Jesus said to me, that "HE is the resurrection and the life. He who believes in HIM will live, even though he dies" (John 11:25). The *Life* that sprung up in me after *Death* was the WORD of the LIVING GOD. The life that is in the WORD has been proven to reign even in the midst of death. If the WORD is in you and you are in it, therein lies the opportunity for not just *life*, but *LIFE* more abundantly. One can die a thousand deaths but will be resurrected from them all because of the WORD. Through these experiences, life has taught me what it really means to follow Christ. It doesn't mean that I have to perform a perceived perfection, meaning to "act" as if I have it all together, or to "look" a certain way to people while exercising the learned behaviors of the "fake it til you make it" ways of the world. To be of the world means to become a master of the facades, charades, or theatrics of what *people* think is "good", "acceptable", or "right". To follow Christ, from my perspective, means that I walk with HIM just as I am. While I transform into truthfulness and tact, changing the way that I think by first renewing my mind through the WORD of GOD to gain the ability, sensibility, and maturity to *BARE WITNESS* to all my faults, iniquities, and transgressions so that I may learn myself and know that which is good and acceptable to CHRIST and *not* people. In HIM, I have the freedom to be who I am and allow correction and perfection to come through His WORD.

JURY INSTRUCTIONS. Members of the jury, you have seen and heard all the evidence and arguments presented in these cases. You have two duties as a jury. Your first duty is to decide the facts from the evidence in the case. Your second duty is to apply the law that gives you the facts. You must follow these instructions, even if you disagree with them. Each of the instructions is important, and you must follow all of them. Perform these duties fairly and impartially. Nothing that is said now, and nothing said or did during the trial, is meant to indicate any opinion about what the facts are or about what your verdict should be. The defendant is presumed innocent unless and until the defendant is proven guilty beyond a reasonable doubt. The burden is on the Courts to prove the guilt of the defendant beyond a reasonable doubt. Reasonable doubt is doubt based on common sense and reason and means an honest uncertainty as to the guilt of the defendant. Reasonable doubt exists when, after careful and impartial consideration of all the evidence in the case, you are not convinced to a moral certainty that the defendant is guilty. The Defendant is never required to prove his/her innocence or to produce any evidence at all. If you find from your consideration of all the evidence that the Defendant committed one or more of the above acts beyond a reasonable doubt, then you should find the Defendant guilty. A unanimous verdict, meaning all twelve of you must agree on a verdict, is required. The Court thanks you for your attention to this important matter. Deliberation may now begin…

DELIBERATION (SELAH). In the beginning was the WORD and the WORD was with God, and the WORD was God. In Him was life; and the life was the light of men. And the WORD was made flesh and made His home among us. He was full of unfailing love and faithfulness. And we have seen His glory, the glory of the Father's one and only Son (John 1: 1,4,14). For God so loved the world that He gave His only begotten Son, that whosoever believed in Him should not perish, but have everlasting life (John 3:16). For our sake He made Him who knew no sin *to be* sin for us, that we might become the righteousness of God in Him (2 Corinthians 5:21). For at just the right time, while we were still powerless, Christ died for the ungodly (Romans 5:6). He was delivered over to death for our sins and was raised to life for our justification (Romans 4:25). He was pierced for our transgressions, He was crushed for our iniquities; the punishment that brought us peace was upon Him, and by His stripes we are healed. All of us, like sheep, have strayed away. We have left God's paths to follow our own. Yet the LORD laid on Him the sins of us all (Isaiah 53:5-6). Therefore, just as one trespass brought condemnation for all men, so also one act of righteousness brought justification and life for all men (Roman 5:18). I tell you, everyone who sins is a slave to sin. A slave is not a permanent member of the family, but a son belongs to it forever. So if the Son makes you free, you will be free indeed… (John 8:36)

THE VERDICT. On indictment of cases presented from 1977 to 2018, charging the defendant Krystal Denise Carr Galloway Wheeler Thomas with criminal acts and intentions from the effects of rejection, promiscuity, low self-esteem, self-doubt, unworthiness, poverty, and death; what say you sir foreperson is the defendant guilty or not guilty… We the jury and cloud of witnesses, in the case of the LAW versus the beloved of GOD (Krystal), find the defendant… NOT GUILTY! 🎶 Let the church say, AMEN (sang Marvin Winans)!

CHAPTER 8:
Life *is* Purposed, Purpose *is* Life
New Beginnings

CASE DISMISSED. "...And we know that all things work together for good to them that that love God and are called according to His purpose" (Romans 8:28). GOD through Jesus Christ, the restorer of my soul, eternally declared "There is therefore NOW, no condemnation to them that are in Christ Jesus, who walk not after the flesh, but after the Spirit. For the law of the Spirit of life in Christ Jesus hath made me free from the law of sin and death"(Romans 8:1). In the face of *DEATH*, GOD, through His Son Jesus Christ, has delivered and liberated me.

In this trial (formal examination of evidence before the judge; test to assess suitability) DEATH was the last enemy to be defeated. Through no power or source of my own was I able to compensate the wages of sin. "For the wages of sin is death, but the gift of God is eternal life through Jesus Christ our Lord" (Romans 6:23). However, the WORD intercepted and interceded and allowed GRACE (delivery of that which is undeserved) and MERCY (withdrawal from that which is deserved) to follow me ALL the days of my LIFE, in the presence of even the last enemy. With the presentation of the facts, including a confession, in this case, a GUILTY verdict was inevitable. The magnitude of the penalty that was laid to my charge carried a weighty sentence. One punishable by death, but 🎶Mercy said "No, I'm not going to let you go, I'm not going to let you slip away, you don't have to be afraid, Mercy said no. Sin will never take control, life and death stood face to face, darkness tried to steal my heart away. Thank you, Jesus, Mercy said NOOOOOO!!! (Saaaannnng CeCe Winans).

COURT ADJOURNED. When I was 🎶"alone in my sorrow and dead in my sin, lost without hope with no place to begin your love made a way to let mercy come in, when death was arrested, and my life began" (sing North Point). The very thing that tried to arrest and condemn me was arrested, tried, convicted, and sentenced itself. Because of the love that is GOD in Christ Jesus, I can boldly ask the questions "Oh Death where is thy sting? Oh grave, where is thy victory? (1 Corinthians 15:55). The RESURRECTION and the LIFE stepped in and breathed into a dead situation, allowed old things to pass away and caused all things to become new. A new creation given a new experience, doing a new thing, in a new life. A complete paradigm shift and transformation of an old mindset. The simple things in life changed to greater things. There was an enlarging of my territory like never before. I learned that perspectives immediately change depending upon the position we *choose* to abide in. When my perspective changed from a selfish to a selfless view, I began to see just how insignificant my worries were, when compared to the PURPOSE of the trials! It is so beneficial to be seated in heavenly places with Christ to view things as HE sees them. His ways are not our ways and His thoughts are much higher than our thoughts. In fact, His ways are beyond our finding out, but if you *remain* in HIM and allow HIS mind to be in you, your steps *are* ordered, and it is in that place where you are able *to taste and see* that He is good.

LIFE IS PURPOSE(D). It is true that my steps have led me into some challenging places. It is also true that I have gone astray, and the detours led to *dead* ends. At times I'm ordered into hills and led into valleys. Other times I run for the hills and fall into the valleys, yet HE remains God of them all. 🎶 "On the mountains, I will bow my life to the one who set me there; in the valley, I will lift my eyes to the one who sees me there; When I'm standing on the mountain aft, didn't get there on my own. When I'm walking through the valley end, no I am not alone! You're God of the hills and valleys!" (sing to my soul Tauren Wells of living water).

My life's path has often looked bleak and troublesome, but the Lord has delivered me from all my afflictions. I have no other choice but to *trust* Him, that's all I can do. For He knows the plans that He has for me, plans to prosper me and not to harm me, to bring me to an expected end (Jeremiah 29:11). Not "the end," that I expect, but an end that He established before my time in and on this earth began. God proclaims, that HE is the Alpha and the Omega; the beginning and the end. It is sustained that... HE IS THAT HE IS. Consequently, the middle will be unclear, but it is that midpoint that requires our "purpose(d)" participation. The central point of life is usually represented by a dash (to run or travel somewhere in a great hurry) as it is marked by a certain beginning date and a set end date. What we do in our dash (run/travel) as we pass between the two parts determines the course of our natural life and the continuation of our eternal life. 🎶 "Who can I run to, to fill this empty space, who can I run to when I need LOVE (surely God will provide an ESCAPE; sang XSCAPE!).

Decisions, decisions… they are the keys to life's mysteries. The choices made will determine the course and mode of our progression or digression. WILL we choose the path of righteous for HIS name sake? Or WILL we choose the path that leads to death and destruction? WILL we soar, run, or walk ; or WILL we scurry, creep, or slither? "See, I have put before you today life and prosperity, death and destruction" (Deuteronomy 30:15), choose whom you will serve.

That "Daily Double Jeopardy" question was presented to *him* in the exit interview. Since the initial interview was not beneficial, I had to find a way to make up for my shortcomings to collect information to use going forward… What modality of transport is your life going… question interrupted with a hasty outburst, " I'm going the wrong way!" Of course, he wasn't responding to the question because I had yet to complete it. But funny how that seemed to be the proper response… "sorry", he says. "What's the question?" Again, I formulate the sentence, "what mode of transport is your life going in right now? Are you soaring, running, walking, scurrying, crawling, or slithering? I patiently waited on the other end of the phone as he constructed a response that would target me and/or our relation*shit*. His response, "well, I was crawling but now I'm running". Just as I anticipated, an answer given as to imply that I slowed him down and I no longer hindered him from moving freely and swiftly… Next question… Why was that your choice, why run and not scurry? I prompted. "What's the difference between running and scurrying?" The reply to that question let me know that his previous answer was chosen out of a place of familiarity. He lacked an understanding of the other choices so he unconsciously refused new information to perhaps make a more sensible selection. As the conversation progressed through his confusion after the new information was fed to him, he couldn't determine whether he wanted to run or scurry. "Ok, I think I'm running because I have a plan all mapped out and I am following that plan". MY THOUGHTS: Oh, now there is a plan when there was not an inkling of a plan or anything mapped out for the duration of our time together. In fact, there was a lot of instability and indecisiveness. Again, he frantically blurted out, "I'm going the wrong way". I don't believe in coincidences and this in no wise was one. The Word says out of the mouth of two or three a thing is established. He was answering the question "in spirit and in truth" when he answered unaware. Surely, God was in this place and I knew it, but he didn't. The last response was a perplexed and unscripted "Am I going the right way?" ... and a then he hastily said, "I'll call you back," as he struggled to determine his natural direction while unknowingly revealing his spiritual direction.

"You can get with this or you can get with that… and of course the choice is yours" (spit it Black Sheep) . If you choose the way of the Lord, *will* you wait upon Him to renew your strength and mount up with wings as eagles when trials come? *Will* your feet be beautiful as they run the race set before you with endurance, to tell of the good news, and finish the course? *Will* you walk in obedience even through the valleys of the shadows of death, fear no evil and faint not because you know that He is with you? If death and destruction is the path of your choice, you *will* scurry to mischief as your heart turns away from the truth. You *will* creep upon the earth as you are drawn away by your own lustful appetite. You *will* slither through the trenches of life as you bow down to other gods and worship them. We all have a right to exercise our own *"will's"* or we can trade our "will's" for His "WILL". "For I command you today to love the LORD your God, to walk in obedience to Him and to keep His commandments, decrees and laws; then you will live and increase, and the LORD your God will bless you in the land that you are entering to possess" (Deuteronomy 30:16). Now, choose life…

Oftentimes decisions are made without having sufficient information. Hosea 4:6 proclaims "My people are destroyed for lack of knowledge (information); because we have rejected knowledge". Let me just say that it is impossible to get "in formation" without obtaining the proper information… "Okay ladies now let's get in formation" (sang Bey). Information about how we should live when we choose life is scripted for us in the Book of Life (The Holy Bible). It also comes from the experiences that God allows us to walk through. So many times, we scurry through the same cycles and repeat unnecessary experiences because we conform to the patterns of this world instead of being transformed by the renewing of our minds through the Word of God and those experiences. If we continue in this state, not acknowledging (obtaining and acting on the knowledge thereof) God, there is a strong possibility that we *will* succumb to every self-pleasing thought without considering the Word of God. This state of mind is called reprobate… (re- again; probate- unprincipled established validity of a will). In other words, it is the re-establishment of a dead man's *will*. Once we have exchanged our *will's* for HIS Will we should "throw off every weight that slows us down, especially the sin that so easily trips us up" (Hebrews 12:1).

When we allow our own desires to take over, we are inevitably drawn away from the word, character, and mind of God and follow after our natural state mind and satisfy the things of the flesh instead of the spirit. "But every man is tempted, when he is drawn away by his own lusts and enticed (James 1:14). Consequently, because I was one who enjoyed sex… yes, I enjoyed sex! Often, I allowed "it" to lead me, lure me, and almost consume me as I constantly gave into the temporary thrill, and nonchalantly dismissed the deliberate effects. The sex didn't heal me, it didn't console me, it didn't renew me…. But it KEPT me mentally and physically enslaved to relational stagnation. However, I knew and understood that there was more to my life than sexual satisfaction… I needed more, I yearned for more, and I realized God's purpose for me required that I understood the things that caused me to deviate from God's intended course for my life.

There were many times that I've refused new information and chose to remain in ignorance. Some think that ignorance is just not knowing, but it goes a bit deeper than that. The root word of ignorance is ignore (to refrain [willingly] from noticing or recognizing). Therefore; it's not just not knowing, it's having the opportunity to know and choosing to remain unaware. Ignore it, then it will go away has been the answer to so many of my life's situations. If you are honest, it's been the answer to some of the things in your life as well. In ignorance, even though I was a woman "I talked like a child, I thought like a child, I reasoned like a child"; but when I stopped ignoring that fact and began recognizing that I was a WOMAN, I put the ways of a child/girl behind me (1 Corinthians 13:11). " I am woman, hear me roar, in numbers too big to ignore, and I know too much to go back an' pretend 'cause I've heard it all before, and I've been down there on the floor. No one's ever gonna keep me down again. Oh yes, I am wise but it's wisdom born of pain. Yes, I've paid the price, but look how much I gained.

If I have to, I can do anything. I am WOMAN hear me roar. You can bend but never break me, 'cause it only serves to make me. More determined to achieve my final goal ,and I come back even stronger not a novice any longer ,'cause you've deepened the conviction in my soul, we are women, hear us roar (sang Helen Reddy).

Let us come out from among them, them being strange women, foolish women, silly women and let us become virtuous women, wives, and mothers. Ones that choose LIFE on this day that heaven and earth can **Bare Witness** with our choice so that us and our children may live (Deuteronomy 30:19).

CONCLUSION: We live and then we leave… imprints of our physical are captured on a single scroll, each loose leaflet sheet of paper tells our story; one word and one year at a time. It doesn't matter how short or how long your book is , what matters is the impact and influence of **your story**… SO, give yourself permission to ***BARE WITNESS!***

Bare Witness:
Mask Off

About the Author

Krystal Carr is simply a small-town girl living in this lively world. A world in which life doesn't necessarily go as planned. Consequently, it will take us by surprise. This concept has proven to be the bane glory of her existence; beginning with her accidental, but God purposed service within public education. Krystal received her Masters' Degree in Educational Leadership from Saint Leo University. She has served behaviorally challenged students as a professional educator for nearly two decades.

Although, her dream(s) did not include caring for children other than her own, her *purpose* superseded her *plans*. She is compelled to love the [seemingly] unlovable and Krystal understands the language of ill behavior. Her nurturing persona and tender heart have left a loving impression with everyone she encounters. Krystal purposely & continually strives to be ALL that God has ordained her to be!

www.ingramcontent.com/pod-product-compliance
Lightning Source LLC
Chambersburg PA
CBHW071216070526
44584CB00019B/3045